Asleep in the Orchard Grass

Asleep in the Orchard Grass

Poems by

Daniel Spees

Foreword by Christopher Howell

WOODLEY MEMORIAL PRESS

Acknowledgements

Thanks to the editors of the following journals in which these poems, sometimes in earlier versions, were previously published: *Big Hammer*, "Alcoholism"; *Coal City Review*, "Learning to Stand"; *Double Entendre*, "The Snowman"; *The Midwest Quarterly*, "Beyond Matfield Green"; *Mikrokosmos*, "Aspens" and "The Garden Begins to Open Itself"; and *Quivira*, "The Diver."

Kansas Voices published "The Bargain" in 2006.

"The Bargain," "The Garden Begins to Open Itself," "How the World Looks to Michelangelo's David," "Just Rewards of Ambition," "Learning to Stand," "The Snowman," and "Some Lawns" appeared in *Michelangelo's Snowman*, Oil Hill Press, 2006.

To two friends I am especially grateful: Bill Sheldon for his excellent editorial work, and Chris Howell for his reflections on the book and many years of guidance.

Copyright © 2008 by Daniel Spees

Published by Woodley Press
Washburn University
Topeka, Kansas 66621
All rights reserved

Book design by Trey Morgan, Bill Sheldon, and the author
Cover photo by Nia Russell-Spees
Author portrait by Benjamin Spees from a photo by Alan Montgomery

Printed in the United States of America

First Edition

ISBN 0-939391-43-0

for Nathaniel

Contents

Foreword by Christopher Howell	x

BEFORE ALL POSSIBILITY

The Diver	3
Abraham and Isaac Prepare for Winter	4
The Surrender	5
Lake	6
The Snowman	7
Levitation Music	8
Last Call at the Lucky Saloon	9
Lose My Balance	10
Crossing	11
Proverbs for Otherwise Defeated Men	13
Aspens	15
Alcoholism	17
Nestlings	18
The Factory's Address Remains the Same	19
What the Sheep Said	20

LIGHTNING AMONG THE LIVING

Sonnet Abstract: Love	29
Beyond Matfield Green	30
Just Rewards of Ambition	31
Front Stoop, 2 a.m.	33
Small Astronaut	34
Learning to Stand	35
Coffee	36
Asleep	38
Iowa	39
The Beauty of Winter	40

Window on the First Noble Truth	42
Solace	44
Brown Dwarfs	46
Seeing the Last Sun	47
Harness	49
Brine	51

ONE MORE DISTANCE

Some Lawns	55
The Garden Begins to Open Itself	56
Baudelaire Changes His Stripes	58
Dear Diary	60
Pine Boughs	61
Affection for the Rain	62
Surface	63
Driving from Father's House	64
By the River	65
The Bargain	66
The Homage Brothers	67
Nobody Was Expecting It	68
The Earwax Museum	69
The Tiber, the Spring, the Swamp	70
How the World Looks to Michelangelo's David	72
God Goes Fishing	74

Foreword

I have known Dan Spees in most of his many incarnations. As a National Merit Scholar from a high school almost too small to see; as a terminal temp employee in Seattle; a graduate teaching assistant; a long haul trucker; a father and step father of a large and varied family; as a theology student; and a gifted college teacher. In all of these roles what most clearly defines him for me has been his spectacular intelligence.

It is no surprise, therefore, to find it in these graceful poems from which the speaker looks upon a world both beauteous and fallen. The songs of crickets, a sudden pandemonium of birds in a field, the sheer physicality of dailyness, these are brought to us with a patience and fearless understanding that lends the poems an authority beyond that which most first books can invoke. What the speaker says he does not say lightly, and yet the poems in this book are full of lightness. No one would call these imagist poems, yet the images here are as true to our experience of the world as images can possibly be.

The poems of fatherhood and love sparkle with plain clarity and announce that Daniel Spees has at last found his way to what he was meant to be: a giver of gifts, a poet. And, though his are not pastoral poems, necessarily, the best way to read them is to imagine Dan seated next to you on a bench on a small rise that overlooks a field and then, as you read, to listen to this strong, honest, beautifully modulated voice. It is an intimate, joyful voice, too, full of that grieving which is joy's inescapable handmaiden, full of invitation, and passionate regard.

I feel privileged to know this poet, and honored to introduce *Asleep in the Orchard Grass* to readers hungry for poems that will not evaporate, like snowflakes, as you read them, that will stay in the ear and the heart and be most intelligent and affectionate company.

Christopher Howell
April, 2008
Spokane, WA

Before All Possibility

The Diver

Tropical fish
swim by and I look at my photo album.
Cigarette smoke wavers like the leaves
of undersea plants. Here is a picture

of my father, black pipe
wedged in his mouth.
A gray dolphin cruises through the room
with muscular
gestures of tail. In this shot,

my mother on a green blanket
eats nectarines. She was a lovely girl
with eyes like nickels.
And in this one, my own eyes
look up at me from a child's chubby face
and a blue canvas chair,

my legs stuck out like oars.
Untold tons pressure
me to my chair. I turn another page and
the arms of the squid embrace me.

Abraham and Isaac Prepare for Winter

My father bought the frame
of a U-Haul trailer, sided it
with plywood, and painted
it aquamarine. One of the boys
at the lodge told him
where to find the bone yard
of a forest fire.
He could cut all the wood
he'd need to keep me splitting all winter.
Sawing a gray tree on the gutted slope,
sawdust stuck to his cheeks,
he slipped and whisked some skin
from his calf, *Jesus H. Christ!*

The broken deadfall
was so thick we stood in kindling
to our shins. He shoveled
it in around the stove-lengths.

His back to me,
the shovel resting on his shoulder,
another order came to mind.
When he turned he drew a red line
across my neck. *Just a scratch.*

The Surrender

When Dad's Dodge gave up
on the I-70 summit of the Rockies
I let it coast to the next
exit. Standing by
the car, my face
reflected in the window
didn't look worried,
although there was only one
cigarette left in a flattened pack.
My blue jeans hung
from my hips
like a defeated hammock.
Right then I was sorry
I'd told Dad all about
the angels I'd seen,
how they shucked the guise of pigeons
at the library,
or stood in blue caftans on the machine-
shop floor.
I wasn't sorry yet that I'd gone crazy—
I didn't know—
but that was why he'd given me the car.
To keep me out of the rain.

Lake

It was precisely in the center of summer.
My girlfriend's cousin had a cabin
    up in Reading, right by the lake.
  So, with blankets and towels
  in a cardboard box

we rode weekends to this shack on the shore
where there was a porch, cots, and a kerosene
    lamp, an outhouse listing left,
    hammock between pines, cistern,
    matches, clothespins, sandals.

The loneliest lake in the county,
my girlfriend's fat cousin said
    between the waves, whispers,
    chuckling noises of the insects,
    water, and trees, and my girlfriend
    laughed about it until dark.

The loneliest lake maybe in Kansas,
she murmured in my ear beside me
    on the creaking canvas. At ten o'clock
    the water went black except for splashes
    of moonlight. Her thighs were
    cool slick lotion on my sunburned hide,

like memory, like lake sounds interrupting
as I lecture my kids.

The Snowman

I wonder how my town,
there, brown and away
in fading light,
looks to the falling snow.
Gray arms of trees
reach into the sky.

Yellow lights flare
one by one as the flakes
spiral toward town. I can think of my body
as disparate crystals,
each one as carefully filigreed

as a Tiffany lampshade. My body sifts
through vaults of air,
alights everywhere, silences the streets,
stretches out along branches,

on the tops of walls.
My girlfriend says
that though I am deep
and quiet,
I am cold.

Levitation Music

The longer I play
my guitar
the higher she rises,
arms stretched
out and back, losing
a russet cardigan.
It hangs between
her wrists like bunting.
Flag of fire
orange hair snapping
in a stiff blast.
Power lines sag, suspension
bridges loaded with snowy
pilgrims bound
for the shrine
at the top of the pole.
Flakes dance in the blue
lamp cone.
She twists and writhes,
calico slipping up her thighs,
up past the steeple,
over the sycamore tree,
a dot against the cloud shine.
My fingers
bleeding on the strings—
but she's too high now—
what if I stop?

Last Call at the Lucky Saloon

Bees well out of twilit trunks.
I stoop to gather

and cover tomorrow with maps
of Nebraska and bits
of foil. The clouds

are hammered rafters between which
a cat reclines in the blue
before all possibility.

I pass through the tabernacle
of a tree-lined street
having poured libation
and received communion.

Lose My Balance

I leave Gina's apartment at 1:00 a.m., higher than I thought. The grass is spongy from constant rain. Somebody is following me. The Burger King sits a lake of asphalt away: reflective panes and steel. Its playground, wrapped in netting, is a huge and sinuous cantaloupe. Metal street signs speak under their breath. If I run, I will lose my balance. A black dog eyes me impassively from the grass a hundred yards away. My skin smells the sweet carrion breath. My bones rebel. My heart sends heat to the lungs and steam to the lips. I can see veins throbbing in the pavement. My apartment hunches up to me like a fat man in a winter coat, and the hilt of the key refuses to budge the bolt.

Crossing

Right at 7:34,

like always, like it's
just supposed to be that way,

the railroad crossing
lights begin to flash

like intense little flames
or angry eyes.

They planned it
like that, *just to bring
me up short*, that's what
I sometimes think,

but I unclench my teeth and fists
and light a cigarette.

It tastes
like coming home,
the tang of spiced
cider, biting
my tongue, a 9-volt

battery, the vinegar
on cabbage, the stinking, delicious
funk of a lover's

sweat, of an overripe
peach, even the swig
of antacid

chasing the morning's
first beer.

Proverbs for Otherwise Defeated Men

The eyes jerk,
the lips will not be a party
to Friday. It seems
every hour bland fat guys promise

to quit eating in offices. They won't
give their names,
or numbers,

and they don't lend money
from rocking chairs and
a roommate would seem like a crowd.

If they need to
phone they do it
from the corner store
where they can stand

and watch the invitations of women
pass them by
because it only costs a quarter

and later they get drunk.

Tuesday is movie night, bathrobe night.

It's better to live in a building—

you don't mind the neighbors.
Cowboy hats, cigarettes, and bad checks,
it all goes together,

at least that's the wisdom.

Aspens

The day swims
in and out as I lie
in my Saturday bed, in my blue
sweats and T-shirt.
I have nowhere
to go but sleep.

I am dreaming of a green
bird darting through a dark forest,
past a circle of marble columns,
then a black cloud
takes me to the mountains,
bird, stone, and vapor,
a wheel carrying my heart away
to a far, cold country
where the people wear heavy boots.

Today I go to the movies,
a story of a man who stands by the ocean,
beaten by time.

I am dreaming about a thin river
that winds through the mountains
and shines pale silver in the sunlight.
The goats come down to the edge

and drink the cold water.
They are invisible goats
so I can see the water move along
their throats right into their bellies.
I fall a long way into the aspen
branches, I watch the smoke rise
from a nearby village
where they bake good bread.

The sun sets before
I can leave the theater,
and rain is falling,
which I always find a cause for celebration,
although nobody seems to love it
that water just falls from the sky.
Something we need so badly
and that we mostly are
just falls out of the air
trying to find our upturned mouths
and pale silver rivers.

Alcoholism

Alone in my apartment
I drink the last of the three
beers I have, a faint humming in my skin,
my belly burning
almost unpleasantly.
Never again, I swear,
will I drink
without the money to buy enough,
though maybe I should
swear off altogether.
But I've taken
that oath more than once,
making my buddies, fellow barflies,
nod indulgently.
They've heard it before,
said it, too.
He'll be back, they think.
As if it matters.
There's always somebody on the next stool.
Every day I play a game
of pool, have a smoke,
desire an end to the misery.
Every day I desire a black-haired girl
who will kiss my fat belly
and sit with me at movies.
But right now I think
I'll go next door
and cadge a few bucks from Bob.

Nestlings

The sun runs from me
as I climb the hill.
Sweat leaks from my face like tears.

I see something in the street,
round as the top of a swimmer's head.
It is a nest tossed out of the tree's arms.

Now I will demonstrate
my kindliness, holding
the twittering hearts

of nestlings in
my palms.
But the babies lie

on the blacktop, yellow and bare,
their dead veins
like stopped blue rivers,

bulbous eyes
and hints of wings.

The Factory's Address Remains the Same

The Nordenskjold Sea is an arm
of the Arctic, like God's
in the act of abandoning a comet
to an elliptical course
like yours, trailing
telegrams:

—bomb commemoration today—

—gambled last week—no luggage—home soon—

We arise unrested for work
having signed a yellow-dog contract,
listen to the foreman's skiing sagas,
work extra shifts at straight time.

When will you come back,
barge in and interrupt the desolate monologue
I've prepared for the sunbeam
shining through my beer glass?

Graves open and close
on the earth
like the boiling surface
of a thick stew.

What the Sheep Said

for Natasha

I. THE COLD ROOM

Branches are bare all over town.
The stars drift their gradual circles
across the sky like bright motes.
In the darkness,

children's laughter.
Snow through wind-brushed
alleys heaps against dumpsters.
The neon marquee of the movie house
jitters and stains

the snow hot pink and aquamarine.
At home in my loft, I wash
a canvas in yellow

and black birds appear.
Tea steams in a tin cup.
The sheriff's four-by-four

pushes past my window.
Silent on the couch
you lie reading, a forgotten

hand resting on a fan
of photographs.
I wish I was mist

rising from your lips.

II. THREE HOURS BEFORE DAWN

Among the serene dead, I approach
the river. The lean bodies
and glossy paws of dogs move
through the mountains
and wet grass.

My feet cool
on glistening river clay
and a bird glides
over the water
where spot fires burn between
charred trees.

Sound of a penny whistle
from a swollen boat,
its hull slicked with moss,
drifting toward
my feet. I get in.

III. YOU HAVE ENTERED MY SLEEP

A white bird,
the water's surface,
his shining shadow.

Black orchids kissing.

Under the skin
of a green pool,
black hair washes
your shoulders.
You vanish
beneath a bank of lilies,
appear at the shore lifting
water to my mouth.

I've heard your
stately songs of loss,
stern carriage of head and arms
at odds with your lush mouth.

Your translucent face
turns to smile
at a word.

IV. CONFESSION

When I drop a brick from the brink
of a roof and watch it
end over end,
plummeting,
it's hard not to feel
it's pulling me with it.

A shell
of anguish
drug through each day
is hoisted
onto the wreck of my bed,
and tears press pointlessly
like tethered watchdogs.

Bending to kiss you
seems electrically obvious,
but it's a brass handle
at a penny arcade:
I can't let go.

V. GRACE

Men once
reached
into the burning

bones of trees
thinking they could
hold fire.

She wears wide stripes
of linen. Brass bangles
at her throat,
she reads poems
to an upturned

sheaf of faces,
and she stands like
a slender

stone.
Her eyes move
across the pages

as Chinese carp
glitter in their pool.
The room is nothing

but her voice,
and I am the pale
shadow watching

this grace
that surpasses
even my longing.

VI. THE SONG'S HANDS

The song of crickets
makes the night bearable.

A beetle reaches
the top of a rock,

shell gleaming
in the moon.

A crane considers
along the shallows on one foot.

Another foot.
Trees

on the bank sway together,
horses drink, toss their heads,

and snort. Night bearable
and the crickets singing.

VII. THE OPERATING THEATER

Sleep and a gleaming
dream of steel
and surgeons brilliantly lit.

I sit clamped in a black
chair as they search
my body's text

for the error,
the cipher
that makes my heart.

I see a woman,
a doorway,
a thread

from her skirt.
The dream's sullen phantoms,
the kiss,
the dark bite.

Lightning Among the Living

Sonnet Abstract: Love

Somebody has already said it,
most likely better than you can,

but it hasn't been said by you,

full of death,
rages of passion.

A climax, as it were,
a satisfying resolution.

She is beautiful.

That much is obvious.

Beyond Matfield Green

All the leaves
are down, dead trees
like lightning
among the living. We listen
to afternoon lyrics

and walk a beach
littered with beer cans, Thanksgiving,
and arguments. Our eyes are beads,
wooden in a loop
of subject/object like the hill,
a cheek dotted with kisses, with graves.

Breath wears a glove
of fragility, a creek bed
lined with wool. We cross the hay
field to the gate, kissing ice
off the rocks.

And later,
as we ascend the bridge's shoulder,
the moon a superabundant buttermilk balloon
above the silo, isn't it
the dead who are awake?

Just Rewards of Ambition

Back then when my life was over
I was twenty-two, worked
at a carwash

across a parking lot from a strip
joint. 500 cars
a day in summer, not enough

hours in fall, nothing
but a beer
at Murphy's when I got off

the bus, red beans
and rice when I got home.
I built a cage

in a corner
of my room, but came home
with a rat that birthed

a dozen pink and wriggling
fingers in my bed, and I took it
back to the pet store so that

the cage sat empty under
a mural of what I figured
my skull looked like,

electric and blue under the meat.
Then I worked
at a group home

for the developmentally disabled
and got lost
on the East Side

with eight of them in a minivan.
Enough. Then I went
to grad school

and married a coworker
from my first campus job.
And now a baby's on the way,

so everything's different.

Front Stoop, 2 a.m.

The stars hurt my eyes.
I'm smoking a cigarette
while my wife drowses
at the back of the house.
I slide into a hot bath
and console my skin with soap.
When I extend my legs
into air, the fat slips
like candle wax.
Immersed in the amniotic wash
of my wife's belly, in waters
dark as Carlsbad, someone
else is doing the same.
In the suds,
a shadow of him
grown tall and smarting
under the stars.
Yesterday
his shoulders turned
under my hand.

Small Astronaut

When I held my baby
against my belly
those DNA helixes
tightened down like screws
saying *mine. I* wasn't
mine anymore, but *his,*
and only important
as something between
him and whatever
could hurt any one
of the almost invisible
hairs beneath a first hat,
a short length
of cotton hose closed at one
end with blue tape. Reflex
or not, he gripped my thumb,
and slept, small astronaut,
earth-bound like the rest of us,
nothing like the rest of us.

Learning to Stand

You aggressively shaped your black
mamma's belly and I wonder
what she'd have said had she known
your skinny self
would issue forth as white as me.

Of course her mother was white, a woman
who came home from Philadelphia
to her folks' farm in Kansas
with four mulatto children.
I'm sure your black mamma learned a lot.

There are still days when your mother
can't pick me out from a half
dozen white people in a grocery aisle,
but as you balance

a few precarious
seconds between us
on the living
room rug, I know
she'll never have
that trouble with you.

Coffee

It wasn't the first time
he gave up and merely sat down
to stare, with an empty stomach,
aching head, but he was

held rigid by a picture of fish
and their comfortable cold current
washing woods and meadows
in the frame hanging
on the kitchen wall.
Then he dreamed

of pasture shoulders draped
with cottonwood trees and heat
and flanks of browsing
cattle. True, it was his grave
he was really thinking about,
that turned him to the stink of living,

the towns he wouldn't see,
people who would neither cry
nor think of him.
The percolator
rattled like lungs
and the blood

in the glass
knob consoled, but suddenly
the chain of days snaked
out in front of him

seemed short.
The chair, the cups,
the kitchen floor,
sun pushing dust
around in shafts.
Now and still now.
Nobody was up yet
and the staircase
did not call him.
The coffee sighed
and was done.

Asleep

She lies asleep on her side,
thighs slipping
a white cotton shift,
her head cradled by embroidered blooms,
eyes adjourned,
lips parted.

Five months pregnant,
hair black splashed on the pillow,
sweet drifting in a blue couch.
The curtain bellies, grazes her fingers.

Iowa

The train's lament is audible as the ringing
arms enfold the crossing.
The engine conducts an orchestra
of right angles. I reel through
the successive sharp contrasts
of painted words.
Across the tracks,
a truck comes my way.
Snow blows over the windshield
in plumes like the breath
icing my beard. The perfectly
good atoms of my body
are ruined with vision
and sound. They love what's
wrecking them like rocks
love the sea, like I love my wife
who shudders with disgust
at my stink, the sweat drenching
my beefy face,
the way my very hands move.
She'll end by casting
me off like the train
does distance,
leaving me in parallel halves
hard and flat and cold,
but even in January
you have to think of all that green
corn blanketing the *Iowa*
stenciled on the boxcars.

The Beauty of Winter

She liked it when he talked about snow,
but he wouldn't speak at first,
in spite of her pleading.
She said she couldn't wait for a story.
Wouldn't he at least tell her one?
He said he was far too tired,
how hard speech was
when it was hot outside.
She didn't like to be humored,
but why couldn't he rise to it?
Why wasn't he more kind?
Kindness, he told her, doesn't
fall like snow, according to law.
Tell me, she demanded, why this is so.
Because snow lasts even in the face
of shovels, even of plows.
Snow drifts as high as it wants.
She wanted him to tell it
more like a story. He told her he could
describe Christmas
and feel neither comfort nor joy.
Snow doesn't know from colored lights.
She wanted him to stop then.
She wanted him to smile, and

that was what she asked him, to smile.
He said it's simply useless
to ask the snow to fall upward,
even if you're the wind.
She wanted him to get back
into his newspaper.
He told her it was too late,
that everybody asks for what they want.
She wanted to know what story he would tell.
He started to say the snow
will collect on your grave
like anyone else's.
The beauty of winter, he said.

Window on the First Noble Truth

Every day
after prenatal
class and teaching
freshmen what a narrator

is, before I'm too
hungry to think
and have to patrol
grocery aisles,

wash dishes, reprimand
children, there is a little
window through which

I see everything
I've given up
and the nothing
I'd have if I hadn't.

Through my office windows,
a net of branches,
a spreading squirrel

hotel. From the apartment
I can see a pickup,
some stars,

an empty pasture.
My colleagues don't mind
my simply staring,
but my wife sighs

over dropped socks

and saucers that need handling.
I get most tired
thinking
about the finite
list of days

and what if I spent
them differently.
Everybody dies
and most wait for it
on less than a dollar
a day. The first noble truth
is suffering, after all,

so I stretch out on the bed
where my wife is sleeping.

Solace

Just when it has
seemed she couldn't
bear one more

contraction
stopping her in the market,
one more comfortless
night, often a solace

has come
and relieved nothing

of the pain except
the way she
held it,
for awhile glad

in the foolishness
of hoping
the blinking baby

would redeem
mistaken marriage,
a sister to balance

her sons.
I know there's no solace
that doesn't

whitewash boards
really old and raw.

Tonight we howled and scathed
each other over
a cup left unrinsed,

an endearment unsaid around
the systematic
ruination of lives.

Our voices strident
and relentless,
we attacked
the blank fact
of sharing

what there cannot be enough of.
But often a solace comes

from the inexact net of winter
stars, and from being happy
we have anything worth this anguish,
these demands.

Brown Dwarfs

Astronomers at last
found what theory said
must be there: suns that lack
the fusion spark to ignite, and so remain
burnt umber worlds hiding
secrets, the blaze that might
have been forever
deferred. Your eyes, to be compassed by a human
face, hold in check, in the color of dark,
raw honey, their full and leaping
radiance. A beam of sun slides in
through a half-open window
and appears in a crescent
at your iris's far edge, writes the terrible
horoscope for any world
without you.

Seeing the Last Sun

Ben will be reaching into his breast pocket
for a Marlboro.
I will get my arms around
the curving architecture
of his solid trunk,
broadened from labor,
and hug him back.
We'll walk from my apartment to my office
without one memory of silence,
two alcoholic brothers
being sober together a little,
thinking of this or that day,
laughing at some of them,
doing it all with charity,
pausing to stand with the same angel,
skirting the edge of the Catholic school,
finding a Pre-Mycenaean bottle cap,
recalling eight different women,
embellishing six dirty tricks,
raking our bosses a bit,
being almost tolerant of them, almost serene,
crisscrossing the streets to avoid dogs,
digging graves along the way,
picking a place on the gazebo steps,
the only one with any sun left,
climbing a ramp, frail and noisy,
narrow and cracked, boardwalk across train tracks,
incised eight times by rails,

gleamingly oblivious, like our hands
as they dance with lit cigarettes—both of us thinking
the same thing, each of us hopping
our own freight, both of us telling
the same lame jokes, the city lights blurring,
fences zooming by, like being drunk,
both of us walking to the front steps of my building
so we can sit on a bench, so I can
show him where the gargoyles should be, so we can
look for monkeys in the tame sycamore
branches, the wildness lost—
trees inoculated and trees sedated—
wrapped in the center of a spreading quilt
of barnyards, pastures, hay fields, and towns
laid out in grids regular as the chain mesh
marking a playground—the baler patrols
the field in a constantly diminishing circle
just over the tree line and fifteen streets
from the campus where we sit, leaving one
bristling package after another,
to be hooked onto the flatbed and stacked
in the mow in heart-lurching heat, we sitting there
paring our nails, he with penknife,
me with stainless clippers, standing up
and smelling the hay, walking single file
until we reach the library, singing The Doors
all the way back, grasping at rain patiently,
grasping at wind, walking into the shadow,
seeing the last blue, seeing the last
crow, last sun.

Harness

I remember when it seemed
like the world
wanted me to be
good and believe

in exercise
and drafting resumes.
Sometimes, when sober,
I thought I was

supposed to pray
alone beneath the basement window
to learn God's stern dictates.

My mistake was this choice
between balking
at the harness or buckling

it snugly on when,
of course, there's
nothing
to take or leave.

The lesson should be

that we gain existential dignity
when we recognize the world's indifference,

but since I've already drunk
the cup of coffee that
polysyllabic abstraction
and four bucks
has bought me,
I look at the question
this way: I haven't
had a beer in eight

months, I unbolted
the training wheels
from Junior's

bike and he actually rode

the damned thing,
and God talks
to me every time
my wife smiles or the mail arrives.

Brine

Yesterday I had to meet my wife
after a lecture she attended.
I saw a dog crossing campus
that looked at me like a poised fist.
Dogs used to roam through town
only at night—trotting
the shining pavements after rain,
sniffing the ankles of the late movie line—
but now they bask on the old Highway 11 median strip
and bark to one another down Merchant Street.

    *

The last time I heard music
in this town was when they tore
down the drive-in
and the fluted squawk-boxes
slipped a dying blare of percussion.

I once was caught in my Dodge
in a teller-window line
during the Garden Bounty Parade
and heard the sound of gum
coming free of a Shriner's heel.

*

I can't tell you why I don't play my records
anymore. I should have taken
her and the boys and the baby
away from here back then
when I didn't have all this money tying me down,
to a place where it seems like
a faded billboard on the horizon,
in amber light at 3:00 a.m.,
is barely holding back the brine smell of the sea.

One More Distance

Some Lawns

I'm tired of writing about lawn care,
that green mulch I step in.
Tired of emptying bags of clippings
when the grass itself, the fat blades,
are quite chatty enough, thank you.
And: if-the-lawn-is-growing-what-
is-it-growing-*into*... I'm tired

of the whole darned thing. Every sprinkler
of foreboding. Fertilizer. Flabbiness.
Irony. Laxatives. Pathos.
The ancient gardeners weeded, prayed
and weeded, finally they were done,
threw their trowels in the air, *the air*,
on fire around the tool shed, and

still returned to an amber mug
of beer in the morning.
Checking the mower in the garage; she
conked out the night before, her motor
a swollen heart
with pepper-spots of oil. I may
require a nap after too many

hours, but for now give me another brew.
For now, it promises transcendence
like an Ed Hume column—leafy and green.
The 6th-grade class once left "a thank you note
for the lawn guy at school." It goes like this:
We saw the garden weasel, the gloves, the rake,
the piling place for the compost.

The Garden Begins to Open Itself

I. TILLING

From the nest, hastily built of dead grass,
hanging like a beard, the finch vanishes
in a convulsive racket of wings.

The hoe turns up rags and margarine tubs,
a porcelain insulator, a gear, a bone.
Trees have grown the wire fence into themselves
and wear it like wings.

II. TAROT

The iris leaves stand transplanted
like tarnished swords. In the mower's wake,

upright but headless dandelion
wands shiver, and a cup in earth
remains where the rosebush once was.

Coins of sunlight drop through new leaves
of Maple boughs as the drowned man
rises under the prodding

of the rake. When the flood waters
reach the feet of the wheel-barrow
the empress will walk the south side

of town dressed in the withered skins
of last harvest, the gardener knows.

III. FURNACE

Last frost subtracts into zeroes of rain.
The patch upturned for sunflowers, picked clean
by robins, holds broken sod like a tray

of loaves: under its cold skin the earth burns.
The gardener pulls on soil-crusted gloves
when the rain stops, and though the air is black,

his face blazes in the unearthed light
as he digs. Sweat leaves black tracks on his cheeks,
and the sunflowers grow already.

Baudelaire Changes His Stripes

Compassion, forgiveness, health, charity,
are the light and heat by which the body moves;
man standing in defeat, but also new clothes,
feeds us with enlivening eyes.

We are steadfast, our work is long;
we bear each other hand to shoulder,
we tend each other with soap and cloth,
methodically washing mud-caked feet.

Angels, silently behind us, watch
and set prayers to the music of our blood,
fortifying armatures of spirit
to support any weight of sorrow.

Their fingers smooth our hair with oil
and consoling gestures
despite the ledgers of crimes
stacked against us on sagging shelves.

Volunteers among the famine-wracked,
we force love beyond our limits,
collapse, sleeping at a dusty door,
rasp our breath into the earth.

Communities of angels sing in our limbs—
synchronized, flying, a steady V of geese,
they caress and coax reservoirs untapped;
each time we wake, we smile in our pain.

If rations, blankets, medicine, clothes
have not been released
from our hands, they will be soon,
for our souls, though slow, are certain.

Of all the birds, saints, nurses, servants,
horses and dogs that nuzzle
and work and give and sacrifice and rest
in glorious service,

there is one more just and abundant.
It performs no plays, never struts with pomp,
yet it would die for the least of us,
and unflinchingly stitch all wounds.

It is love, tears tracking its hard face.
You know it as we do. This radiant
lion swells its chest roaring for the weak;
for you, oppressed comrade, my fellow, my brother.

Dear Diary

It was an evening still cold
in March, by a defiled river,
when I heard the midnight
idea expressed in a sentence
that was like a victim staggering,
drooling strands of linked forms.
I held out to it a bouquet of vibrating words
as the moon affixed its foggy disclosure.

Still, it was lovely, the idea,
and it slept, blushing with sex,
slumped on the floor of my master's memory.

Then, too, he recalled how in front of some trees,
a fabulous boy had dragged over his desire,
impatient to sleep and dream himself wonderful,
cleanly, remade among the eroding humps
of farm country.

We stood there, we two, monster
and oaf, writing our obituary operas.

Pine Boughs

Seven gray horses gather
in a misty circle.
Water flows from the mountains

like heavy whispers
of the stones.
Seven gray horses gather in mist

at the shadowy tree line
and stand together almost touching.
Water flows from the mountains

like a road
that leads to a place we remember.
Seven gray horses gather in the mist

of their breathing.
Their muscles shift like
water flowing from mountains.

The horses step,
turn and step, disperse
and gather in the mountains.
Water flows from the mist.

Affection for the Rain

Blue is the color of angels,
a constant reminder

of their absence here
in the flesh, a poor mirror.

Water reflects all right,
so there is one more distance

between us and the sea.
I stood four times

in the mushroom circle
back of my house.

The circle marks the exact
place where the ancient

maple is not: is that not blue
enough, without being washed

by the sky? But the sky
is blue, and so are my eyes,

my protest.

Surface

Feeling for the light
switch, you find instead six
keys on hooks
sunk with linear
insistence into hardwood.
This isn't what you
wanted, but it's better than, say,
a cold arm, or really anything
wet. Also, there are worse things
than having no future.
Look at the dead, for example.
I remember when you wore that yellow hat
the color of the guy I saw
when my dad,
the hospital maintenance man,
gave me a tour, including
the autopsy room.
I used to stuff ashtrays,
and with the butts of real
cigarettes, too—fat, sweet,
whiskey-smelling killers.
That was when I was immortal.

Driving from Father's House

on gravel, her shoulders raking
across some slight,
or unfinished business.
She winked at the lawyer
in the turn-lane,
convivial behind the wheel.
She transcended the road in memory,
and on faith, as if her father
were hung in effigy from the mirror.
The light, the gearshift, the rabbits
beside a median hedge.
Parked at the frayed end of thirty
miles of chalky ribbon,
a violet gown shook her out
naked in the pines,
like someone beautiful, and tired.

By the River

Day by day I rest on the cool banks
and the river sweeps its stony rooms.
I drowse the gliding clouds, without work,
or have a supper of cheese and grapes
on a blanket with the woman
and children I do not know.
Sometimes someone comes
and speaks words,
or the wind does. If the day is clear
and hot, I notice flowers, or even tears.
The heron stilts across the shallows
where the willow hangs her hair.
I can't remember her name.
The parlor the minnows
hang above—turning,
pointing like weathervanes—
is clean now,
all the corners checked,
but the river keeps sweeping,
sweeping, the broom whispers, sweeping.

The Bargain

I don't think
I am as surprised
as I ought to be.
You arrived at the grove,
your boots obscure
with dust.
I handed you a tin cup,
water dripped
from your beard.
I know the country
you were traveling
through, its wasted
trees. Three times
I ascended to the highest
platform of the tower
with my glass.
Finally I *did*
see the cloud
your horse kicked
up, and it is a long
way to come. . .
I can't say more.
Seventy-five dollars
is a lot of money.

The Homage Brothers

In this bunker, we have assembled machines with sheets of loss we felt at the passing of the Great Auk, an erotic bird that knew delicious ice in its secret blubber. The loss is rendered in gossamer cross-sections, packed in gelatin, which quiver and sing to Reykjavik and New Zealand. In keeping with deep sounds and fjords, we inlaid our machines with a filigree of steel valleys and vacuum tubes. The machines are arranged in such a way as to suggest the face in a certain floor tile out there on the landing, though we had to take up the whole bunker floor to manage it. Each machine must be kissed hesitantly, if not with an actual coyness, to kick it over. But if done in the correct order, symphonically, the face will part its gray lips and speak the thirteen words of Magda's poem.

> My eyes delight with
> parrot palm green. In winter
> you stand there, consoled.

We are thought so distant in our lab coats, and, yes, purple shadows do lurk at the corners of our aquiline noses and droop with our pencil moustaches, but where else have you seen such devotion, such grace?

Nobody Was Expecting It

By then the train was away with a cargo of pianos. The first was a woman in Ethic, Georgia: she noticed a new blackness in the sky. A girl in Lostfarthing, North Dakota spent the dinner hour under her brother's bed. In the Shell station's back room, a poker night regular turned and listened to the approaching desert. His yellow cigarette shifted like a compass needle. It stayed quiet until sunup as far as anybody knew. Except, that is, for Chester Halford, who saw a pigeon bank into a Kentucky mortuary's airspace and plummet to the roof.

The Earwax Museum

Our bodies make it;
we could make bodies *with* it.

Blame Descartes
that we inhabit obese *corpi*
like so many ghosts
in sagging Victorian mansions.
I'll give you *res extensa;*
Extend *this*.

The featured piece
in the museum is a study
of René himself.

He kneels at the hearth
with a lump of wax
in his hand.

Changes, but remains
constant. He wore a beanie,
but we show his bald pate.

I hunger,
therefore I am reckless.
The mind and body are one.

The Tiber, the Spring, the Swamp

Hands ring the day's tocsin.
Hands in the rushing Tiber,
        delicate and silent hands.
        Hands in the cienega's vector,
        the old bell hung by the levee.
Hands built the levee,
and the river wears it like a hat.

Can you peel the boughs
and the sorrow of the house nuns love?
        The emperor's love is hermetic,
        a dulcimer's carnation.
The secret peal of the poor secretary's
bell abides entreaty the color of bone.

The chatter of girls and candid blood.
The recurring despair of teeth
        with the purity of weapons,
but love is a weapon, Poseidon's,
a weapon of solitary voice.

But hands, the love of nuns,
incandescences, fill that frame,
        the caricaturist's shifting canvas,
        the emphatic picture window
arranging wooded hillsides.
Enter the lucid and legal instant,

the flame of virtue in a bowl
of lentils. Hands join the suave
        prose of grime, the two
        handles of desolation
        in a secretary's life.
They total a bog of genuflections
that can't be completely recanted.

How the World Looks to Michelangelo's David

Look at all the lights
and colors, say of a great heap
of burning tires, but look without
eyes, because there is nothing
necessary about eyes, the universe
exhales and inhales
regardless. Then smell,

perhaps a fat worm
of mustard clinging to a bit
of cheese, but not with nostrils,
streams of molecules bouncing
spice against the inert air.
Feel the warm dots

of summer rain
chart your face, but feel them
as if built of stone
with nerves like veins of ore.
Listen to the grinding

of sandpaper on coffin
planks. Taste the salt

of sweat that's trickled
along the arched sides
of your nose.
Take it in, but without
even a body, in a universe
that's black,

but not even black (which
implies sight by absence).
How does the world look
to an ingot of lead
or any of the noble gases?

The immense sphere
wobbles through space,
enveloped in oceans of gas,
a complicated sculpture
difficult to perceive
blinded as we are by eyes,
deafened by ears.

God Goes Fishing

(after Philip Levine)

Train whistle moaning out of the dark,
an elkhound at the trestle, the trestle
not drifting into visible space
from the embankment, and winter, and no snow
falling where it fell before.

The old dog in a matted pelt
tells me this is Kansas, this--
he does not say--is the epitome of visible space,
the wide empty plain you get to
after a nervous breakdown,

obesity, liquor, and hate.
He takes off at a slow trot
and the tongue drops from his jaws.
I remember the Tuesday morning
walk to the supermarket,

I saw him lounge on the grass
and growl, and raise
his wedge of a face in cautious scrutiny
of just me. I could tell him that.
I could tell him I was after some doughnuts

or maybe a good cheese.
I could tell him that this isn't
the Kansas I had seen
in movies, or that last night
I saw an old couple laugh,

and not the tired tittering of surrender,
really laugh. We are together

here by the ravine, he and I,
to think it over, the shabby coat of flesh
and the dirt quietly waiting,

and we conclude that we're stuck:
one or two birds that think dawn before us,
no consolation, and no stone notes
from God (whom I imagine
fishing in a straw hat).

www.ingramcontent.com/pod-product-compliance
Lightning Source LLC
Chambersburg PA
CBHW032208040426
42449CB00005B/490